Volcano Rising

Elizabeth Rusch

Illustrated by **Susan Swan**

Charlesbridge

KA-BOOM! Most people think volcanoes are either sound asleep or blowing their tops off in fiery, ash-spewing catastrophes.

But volcanoes are not just destructive.
Much more often, volcanoes are creative.
They grow taller and wider. They form
majestic mountains. And they build new
islands where there were none before.

Both creative and destructive eruptions start with gooey melted rock called magma. Magma from deep in the earth rises up a gigantic strawlike tube to a vent, or opening. If magma makes it to the earth's surface, it's called lava. A burst of lava is an eruption.

Magma is made up of gases as well as melted and partially melted rock. As it rises and fills huge underground chambers, pressure builds . . . and builds . . . and builds . . . until the magma is forced up and out a volcano's vent.

Erupted magma can spurt out and flow down a volcano like red-hot syrup. This fluid lava cools to form either spiky chunks called ʻaʻā (ah-aah) or smooth, ropy surfaces called pāhoehoe (paah-hoh-eh-hoh-eh).

Magma can also burst out in solid chunks called tephra (TEH-frah). Tephra can be tiny bits (ash), lightweight gas-filled pieces (pumice), or solid rocks and boulders (lava bombs).

But what determines whether lava erupts peacefully or dangerously?

ʻaʻā

tephra

lava

vent

pahoehoe

magma chamber

POW! Gases blast lava out in an explosive eruption.

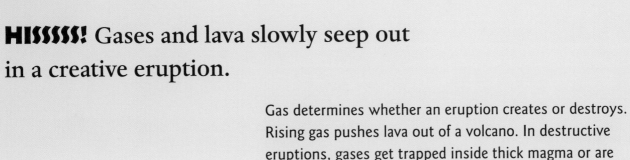

HISSSSS! Gases and lava slowly seep out in a creative eruption.

Gas determines whether an eruption creates or destroys. Rising gas pushes lava out of a volcano. In destructive eruptions, gases get trapped inside thick magma or are blocked by plugs in the vents. Pressure builds until lava, ash, and gases explode all at once, like soda from a shaken can.

In creative eruptions, vents are open and gases escape slowly, like when you carefully unscrew a soda bottle. Lava bubbles and sprays like water from a hose or oozes out like toothpaste from a tube. Layer upon layer of lava piles up, forming lava domes. Over time, peaceful eruptions can build mountains.

Creative eruptions occur three times more often than violent ones. They happen all over the world in all kinds of different places.

North Sister

Middle Sister

South Sister

A creative eruption can start with the ground swelling a tiny bit each year. Magma gathering underground creates a bulge that may one day make a new mountain.

In the Cascade Range in central Oregon, three composite volcanoes—massive cones made from layers of both lava and ash—sit in a tight cluster, as if they're having a tea party. They're called the Three Sisters: North, Middle, and South Sister.

But wait, what's this? A large area next to South Sister rose four inches (ten centimeters) between 1996 and 2000 and continues to rise. This uplift is caused by magma pooling a few miles under the surface. Scientists think a new volcano—West Sister—may join the party sometime, giving us yet another spectacular mountain to explore.

Sometimes creation happens more quickly. Volcanoes can appear out of nowhere! One day the ground cracks and ash spurts out, forming a new volcano.

*Paricutín
(day one)*

In 1943, as a farmer plowed his cornfield in Paricutín (pah-ree-koo-TEEN), Mexico, ash exploded from a crack in the ground and rained down, creating a steep cinder cone. In a day the cone reached 164 feet (50 meters) high. In a week it stood 500 feet (150 meters) tall. Ash slowly buried the farm and nearby villages. But the family and villagers moved to land close by and began farming the rich, ash-fertilized fields.

After a year Paricutín's cone was more than 1,000 feet (330 meters) tall. After nine years the cinder-cone volcano stood more than 1,300 feet (424 meters).

Paricutín is considered one of the wonders of the world. It created a mountain, fertilized fields, and gave scientists the chance to study the fast growth of a new volcano.

Volcanoes even make mountains underwater.
If these submarine volcanoes grow high
enough, their tips form new islands.

Surtsey (today)

Three-quarters of volcanic activity takes place deep in the ocean. In 1963 a submarine volcano near Iceland erupted to create the island of Surtsey. In a few years the island rose more than 550 feet (167 meters) above sea level and grew to be more than a mile (two kilometers) across.

Moss and lichen took hold of the lava rocks. A bush grew and then other plants followed. Finally seals, puffins, and other animals began breeding there.

Surtsey now hosts a small hut for researchers—a new laboratory for watching what happens on a new island.

Some volcanoes secretly erupt under glaciers, hiding growing mountains deep under thick ice.

Grímsvötn (GREEMZ-voe-tihn), Iceland's most frequently active volcano, lies beneath the country's largest glacier, Vatnajökull (VAHT-nah-YUH-koot-ehl), with only a bit of its rim exposed. Underneath the vast ice cap is a hot spot—a place where lots of magma from the earth's mantle rises to the surface. This makes for a very creative volcanic environment, causing Iceland to constantly grow in size.

Creative eruptions can continue for a really long time. **WHOOSH,** fountains of red-hot lava squirt high into the air. **GURGLE,** stinky lava streams to the shore. **TSSSS,** fluid lava hits the ocean, steaming, and hardens to form new land.

For more than twenty-five years, shield volcano Kilauea (kee-lau-WAY-ah) on the Big Island of Hawaii has been in a state of creative eruption. Shield volcanoes have lots of vents, allowing runny lava to leak from cracks to form broad mounds that are shaped like shields.

Kilauea's constant eruption has added more than 500 acres (202 hectares) to the island—that's more than 314 soccer fields! No one works or plays soccer on this new acreage yet. But they will. After all, where would the people of Hawaii live if not for the creative eruptions that helped build all their islands?

Most volcanoes have both destructive and creative eruptions. **WHAM!** They blow their tops. Then **SPURT, GURGLE, SCRAPE,** they get down to the business of building a new dome.

In 1980 Mount St. Helens in Washington State exploded, losing 1,300 feet (396 meters) off its top, shooting a huge black ash cloud higher than airplanes fly, and mowing down massive trees as if they were toothpicks.

Right after the eruption, the volcano began oozing squishy lava pancakes, building a new dome 876 feet (267 meters) high. That's the height of a fifty-story building!

Then, after a thirteen-year rest, the volcano started pushing out huge slabs of hardened lava so fast it could fill a bedroom in a minute. It built a dome higher than the Empire State Building.

Someday Mount St. Helens will completely rebuild its summit, all 1,300 feet—or more.

It's not a matter of *if*; it's a matter of *when*.

lava dome

KABAM-BAM-BOOM!

Even the most dangerous volcanoes—supervolcanoes—can do creative work. Between gigantic eruptions, they can erupt gently for many years, repairing the scarred land.

Hundreds of thousands of years ago, the Yellowstone supervolcano had three gigantic eruptions that blanketed most of the United States with ash. So much magma exploded out from underground that the surface collapsed, swallowing mountains and creating a gigantic crater called a caldera.

Since the last destructive eruption, 640,000 years ago, thirty gentle lava flows have nearly filled in the caldera. Some of these lava flows have been thick and widespread— as large as 130 square miles (340 square kilometers), twice the size of Washington, DC. But the flow oozed slowly, moving at most a few hundred feet per day, smoothing out the land over thousands of years.

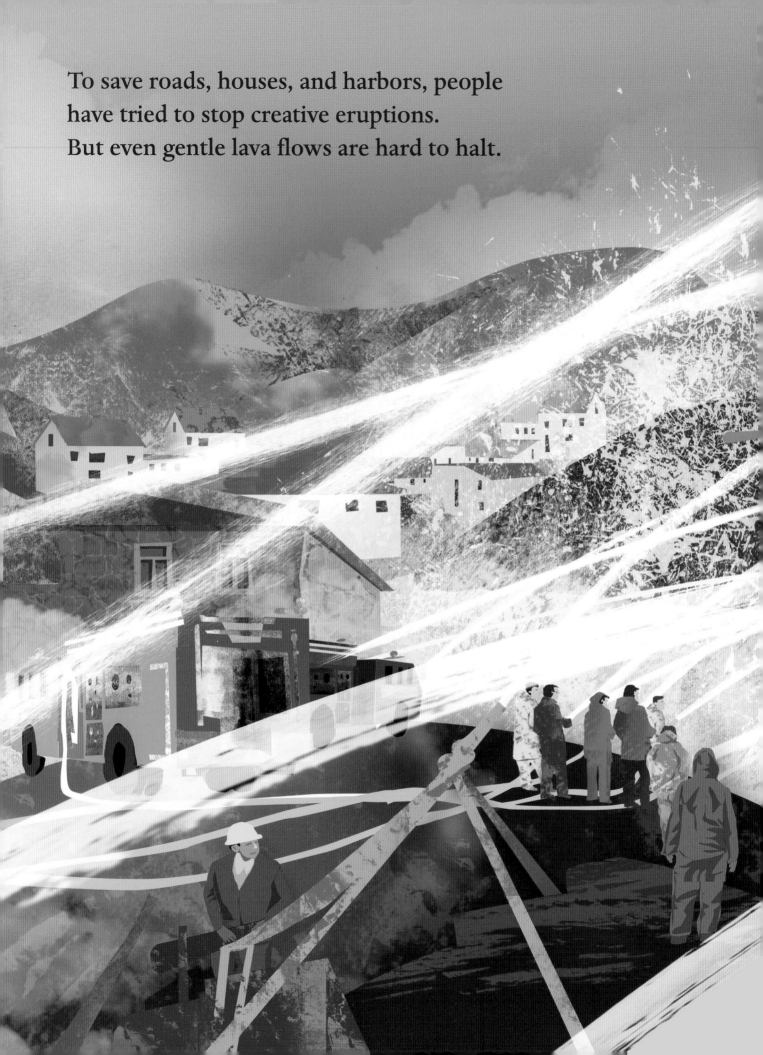

To save roads, houses, and harbors, people
have tried to stop creative eruptions.
But even gentle lava flows are hard to halt.

Heimaey

Engineers in Italy tried to dam lava flowing from Mount Etna. They diverted the flow but couldn't stop it.

The US Army bombed Mauna Loa in Hawaii to redirect lava from the city of Hilo. They missed the target, but luckily the flow ceased on its own.

For five months Icelanders sprayed millions of gallons of water on lava from Heimaey (hay-MYE-ee) volcano, hoping to halt the lava flow by cooling it. They slowed the flow, but still the eruption added one square mile (2.5 square kilometers) of new land to the island and narrowed the entrance to the town's harbor.

Still, people are rarely hurt by creative eruptions because they can outwalk, or outrun, them. In fact, we inch up as close as we can to these eruptions—even underwater— to watch the landscape changing.

Scientists send underwater robots to hover feet from submarine volcanoes, observing ash and pillow lava pulsing from the vent, waiting for an island to be born.

Visitors stroll right up to the bubbling lava leaking out of Kilauea, feeling the heat, squinting at the red-hot glow as an island expands.

Hikers climb to Mount St. Helen's crater rim, smelling the rotten-egg gases, hearing the rumbling of new rocks being made, watching as a volcano rebuilds itself.

pillow lava

submarine
volcano

Creative eruptions give us all a chance
to witness the power of a

VOLCANO RISING!

Volcano Vocabulary

'a'ā (ah-aah): *Hawaiian.* Solid, chunky, sometimes blocky or spiky lava rock formed from a thick, slow-moving lava flow.

active: An active volcano is one that has erupted in the last ten thousand years.

ash: Tiny bits of blasted volcanic rock; see also *cinder.*

caldera: A large pit or crater formed when a volcano collapses into its magma chamber.

cinder: Ash; see also *ash.*

cinder cone: A tall, narrow volcano formed by layers of ash.

composite volcano: A volcano formed by layers of ash and lava; also called a stratovolcano.

crater: A deep bowl formed by either an explosion or a collapse of a volcano.

dormant: A dormant volcano is one that has erupted in historical times but is currently quiet.

eruption: An event that occurs when magma from under a volcano reaches the earth's surface.

extinct: An extinct volcano is one that has not erupted in the last ten thousand years and is not expected to erupt again.

gas: A substance that can expand indefinitely, or if contained can completely fill its container; common volcanic gases include water vapor, carbon dioxide, hydrogen sulfide, and sulfur dioxide.

hot spot: An active volcanic region thought to be fed by hotter-than-normal material coming up from the earth's mantle.

lava: Magma that has erupted to the surface as either liquid or solid rock; see also *pāhoehoe* and *'a'ā.*

lava bomb: Erupted lava chunks larger than 2½ inches (64 millimeters) in diameter.

lava dome: A mound or pile of thick lava that can grow large and steep.

magma: Melted or partially melted rock and gases beneath the earth's surface.

magma chamber: An area that holds melted or partially melted rock and gases beneath a volcano.

mantle: A layer inside the earth above the core (the very middle) and below the crust (the surface).

pāhoehoe (paah-hoh-eh-hoh-eh): *Hawaiian.* Lava rock with a smooth, ropy surface formed by fast-moving liquid lava.

pillow lava: Rounded or mushroom-shaped lava rock formed when liquid lava erupts underwater.

plug: Hardened lava that closes a vent.

pumice: A light-colored volcanic rock so filled with gas bubbles that it can sometimes float on water.

shield volcano: A wide volcanic mound formed when lava flows from multiple vents.

subglacial volcano: A volcano submerged under a glacier.

submarine volcano: A volcano on the ocean floor that has not breached the water's surface.

summit: The peak, or highest point, of a volcano.

supervolcano: A volcano that has measured an 8 on the Volcanic Explosivity Index (VEI), meaning that more than 240 cubic miles (1,000 cubic kilometers) of magma erupted from it.

tephra (TEH-frah): Chunks of lava, large and small, produced by volcanic eruptions.

vent: An opening in a volcano through which lava, ash, and gas can erupt.

Selected Bibliography

Babb, Janet (education and outreach specialist, Hawaiian Volcano Observatory), interview with the author, February 2011.

Brahic, Catherine. "First Subglacial Eruption Found in Antarctica." *The New Scientist* 13 (January 21, 2008): 11.

Driedger, Carolyn, Dan Dzurisin, Cynthia Gardner, Ken McGee, Seth Moran, John Pallister, and Jim Vallance (volcanologists, United States Geological Survey), interviews with the author, 2005–2006.

Foshag, W. F., and J. Gonzalez-Reyna. "Birth and Development of Parícutin Volcano." *US Geological Survey Bulletin,* vol. 965-D. Washington, DC: US Government Printing Office, 1956.

Jakobsson, Sveinn P. "The Surtsey Eruption 1963–1967." The Surtsey Research Society. **http://www.surtsey.is/pp_ens/gen_3.htm**

Koerner, Brendan I. "How Do You Stop a Lava Flow?" *Slate.com* (November 1, 2002). **http://www.slate.com/id/2073445/**

Lauber, Patricia. *Volcano: The Eruption and Healing of Mount St. Helens.* New York: Bradbury/Aladdin, 1986.

Lockwood, J. P., and F. A. Torgerson. "Diversion of Lava Flows by Aerial Bombing: Lessons from Mauna Loa Volcano, Hawaii." *Bulletin of Volcanology* 43, no. 4 (December 1980).

Luhr, James F. (director, Global Volcanism Program, Smithsonian Institution), phone interview with the author, 2006.

—— and Tom Simkin, eds. *Parícutin: The Volcano Born in a Mexican Cornfield.* Phoenix: Geoscience Press, 1993.

Smithsonian Institution, Global Volcanism Program. "Volcanoes of the World." **http://www.volcano.si.edu/world/**

Smithsonian National Museum of Natural History. "Parícutin: The Birth of a Volcano." **http://www.mnh.si.edu/onehundredyears /expeditions/Paricutin.html**

United States Geological Survey and the National Park Service. *Steam Explosions, Earthquakes, and Volcanic Eruptions—What's in Yellowstone's Future?* USGS Fact Sheet 2005-3024 by Jacob B. Lowenstern, Robert L. Christiansen, Robert B. Smith, Lisa A. Morgan, and Henry Heasler, 2005. **http://pubs.usgs.gov/fs/2005/3024/**

United States Geological Survey, Cascades Volcano Observatory. "Three Sisters, Oregon." Information statements, 2002, 2004, 2005, and 2007. **http://vulcan.wr.usgs.gov/Volcanoes /Sisters/**

——, Hawaiian Volcano Observatory. Quarterly Report of the USGS Hawaiian Volcano Observatory, 2006 and 2007.

——, Hawaiian Volcano Observatory. "Puʻu ʻŌʻō-Kupaianaha: Kīlauea's East Rift Zone Eruption, 1983 to Present." **http://hvo.wr.usgs.gov/kilauea/summary/**

——. "Three Sisters Show Ground Deformation." Press release, May 8, 2001. **http://www.usgs.gov/newsroom/article .asp?ID=474**

Wicks, C. Jr., D. Dzurisin, S. E. Ingebritsen, W. Thatcher, and Z. Lu. "Ground Uplift Near the Three Sisters Volcanic Center, Central Oregon Cascade Range, Detected by Satellite Radar Interferometry." In preparation, 2001.

Witze, Alexandra. "Fire and Ice." *Science News* 178, no. 7 (September 25, 2010): 16.

Learn More

Adams, Simon. *The Best Book of Volcanoes*. New York: Kingfisher, 2001.

O'Brien-Palmer, Michelle. *How the Earth Works*. Chicago: Chicago Review Press, 2002.

Robson, Pam. *Mountains and Our Moving Earth*. Brookfield, CT: Copper Beech Books, 2001.

Rusch, Elizabeth. *Will It Blow?: Become a Volcano Detective at Mount St. Helens*. Seattle: Sasquatch Books, 2007.

Smithsonian Institution, Global Volcanism Program. "Worldwide Holocene Volcano and Eruption Information." **http://www.volcano.si.edu/index.cfm**.
Contains archival information about active volcanoes and their past eruptions, as well as up-to-date information about current eruptions around the world.

Text copyright © 2013 by Elizabeth Rusch
Illustrations copyright © 2013 by Susan Swan
All rights reserved, including the right of reproduction in whole
or in part in any form. Charlesbridge and colophon are registered
trademarks of Charlesbridge Publishing, Inc.

Published by Charlesbridge
85 Main Street
Watertown, MA 02472
(617) 926-0329
www.charlesbridge.com

Library of Congress Cataloging-in-Publication Data
Rusch, Elizabeth.
 Volcano rising / Elizabeth Rusch ; illustrated by Susan Swan.
  p. cm.
 ISBN 978-1-58089-408-1 (reinforced for library use)
 ISBN 978-1-58089-409-8 (softcover)
 ISBN 978-1-60734-616-6 (ebook)
1. Volcanoes—Juvenile literature. I. Swan, Susan ill. II. Title.

QE521.3R87 2013
551.21—dc23   2012000793

Printed in Korea
(hc) 10 9 8 7 6 5 4 3 2 1
(sc) 10 9 8

Illustrations created by manipulating found objects, hand-painted
  papers, and scans of objects and textures in Adobe Photoshop
  to create new patterns; adding digital paintings; and then
  collaging the two together
Display type set in NeueNeuelandTF by Treacyfaces
Text type set in Dante MT by The Monotype Corporation plc,
  and Goudy Sans BT by Bitstream Inc.
Color separations by KHL Chroma Graphics, Singapore
Printed by Sung In Printing in Gunpo-Si,
  Kyonggi-Do, Korea
Production supervision by Brian G. Walker
Designed by Diane M. Earley

To the Viva Scrivas. Thank you.
—*E. R.*

For Dr. Richard Swan,
brother extraordinaire.

—*S. S.*